Draw with...
Pablo Picasso

"I don't make speeches.
I talk through my paintings."

Pablo Picasso

F
FRANCES LINCOLN
CHILDREN'S BOOKS

Picasso giving a drawing lesson to his children, Paloma and Claude, and two friends at the La Californie villa in 1957

PICASSO AND CHILDREN

That looks like a Picasso!

Who has never thought this when looking at a child's drawing? Pablo Picasso himself greatly respected children's artwork. He said:

"When I was young I could draw like Raphael, but it has taken me my whole life to learn to draw like a child."

And, like children, Picasso wanted to paint what he felt, even if the resulting painting didn't look very much like what he saw.

Picasso was born in Malaga, in Spain, in 1881. From an early age he showed exceptional artistic ability, especially in drawing. His father, a teacher at the school of fine art, encouraged his son's talent, and at the age of 23 Pablo Picasso left Spain and moved to Paris. There, in the Bateau-Lavoir studio in Montmartre, he began to transform the subjects of his paintings into geometrical constructions freed from the constraints of perspective. In this way his work took its first steps towards the new Modern Art.

Paul Drawing
1923

The Painter and the Child 1969

In 1907 Picasso's famous painting *Les Demoiselles d'Avignon (The Young Ladies of Avignon)* established the beginning of Cubism, one of the most important artistic movements of the 20th century. After the Second World War, Picasso went to live in Vallauris in the south of France with his wife, Françoise, and his children, Claude and Paloma.

Claude Drawing, with Françoise and Paloma 1954

Picasso's children were very often the subjects of his painting during this period and the hours he spent drawing in the company of Claude and Paloma were very important for him. He was fascinated by the way they saw the world, by their freedom and their fantasy. He often said:

"In every child there is an artist. The difficulty is knowing how to hold on to this artist as the child grows up."

Picasso himself never stopped painting and producing art until his death in 1973 at the age of 91.

FACES

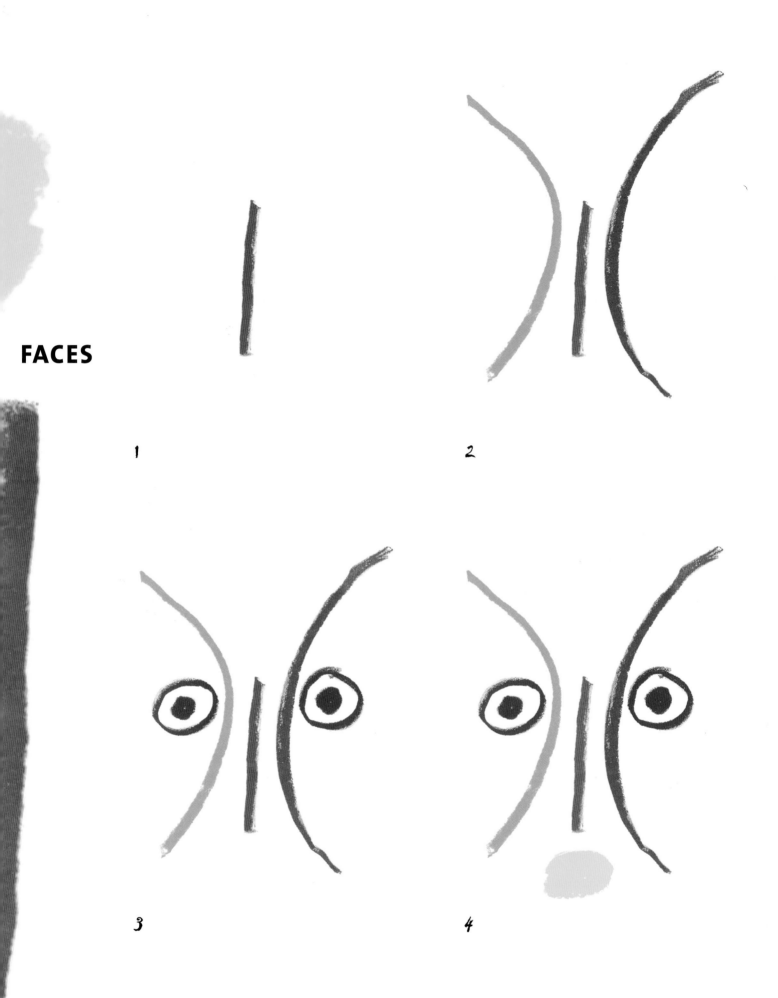

1

2

3

4

"In order to know what you want to draw, you have to start drawing."

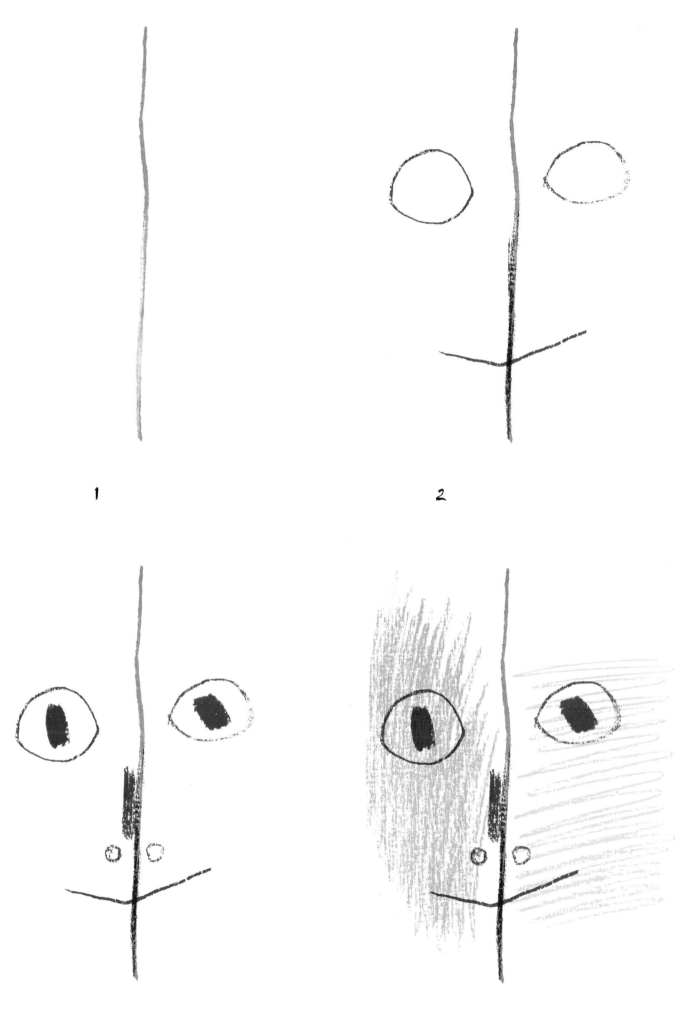

1

2

3

4

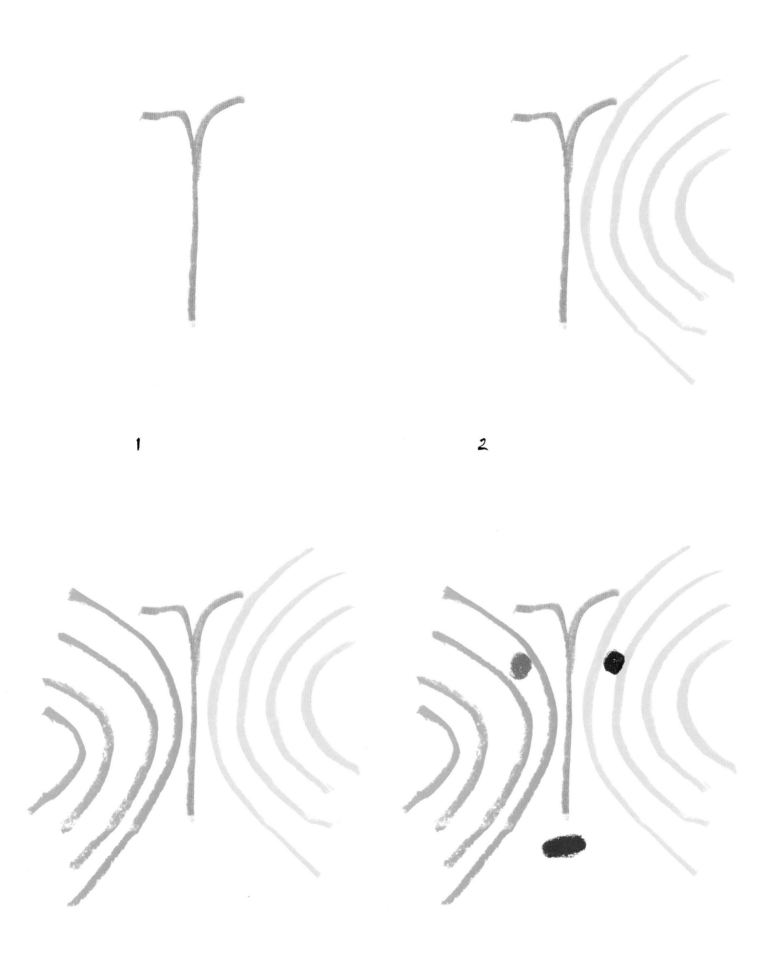

1

2

3

4

"A picture is destined to produce new emotions
in the soul of the person who looks at it."

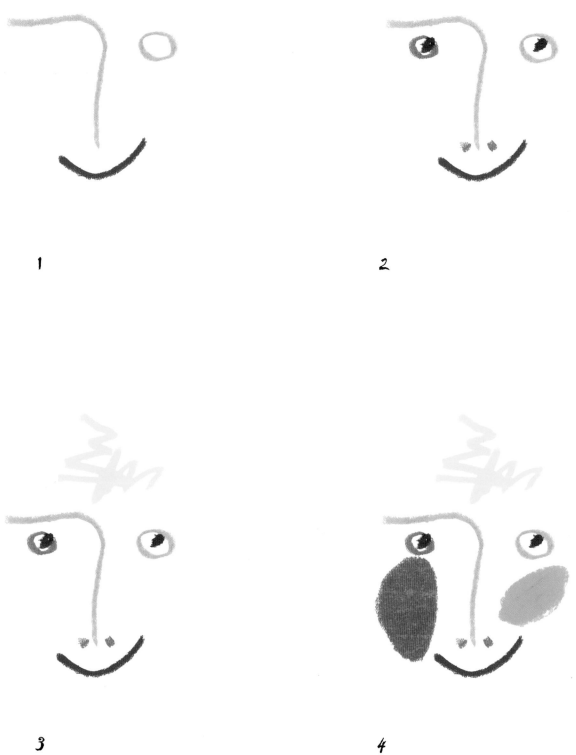

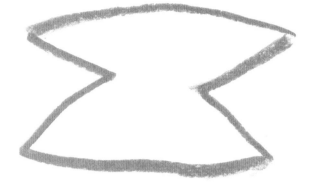

1

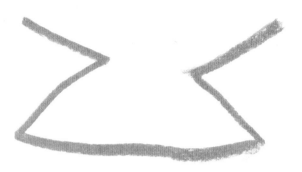

2

3

4

5

6

"When you paint a portrait, there always comes a moment where you have to be satisfied with a sort of caricature."

1

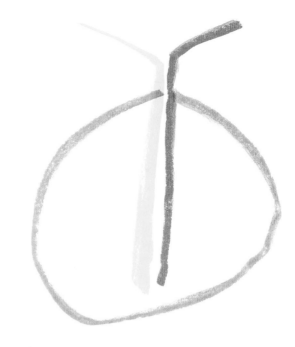

2

3

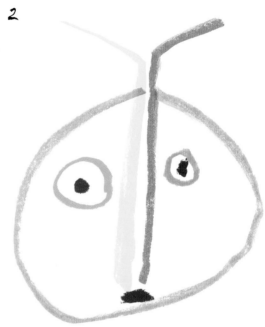

4

5

6

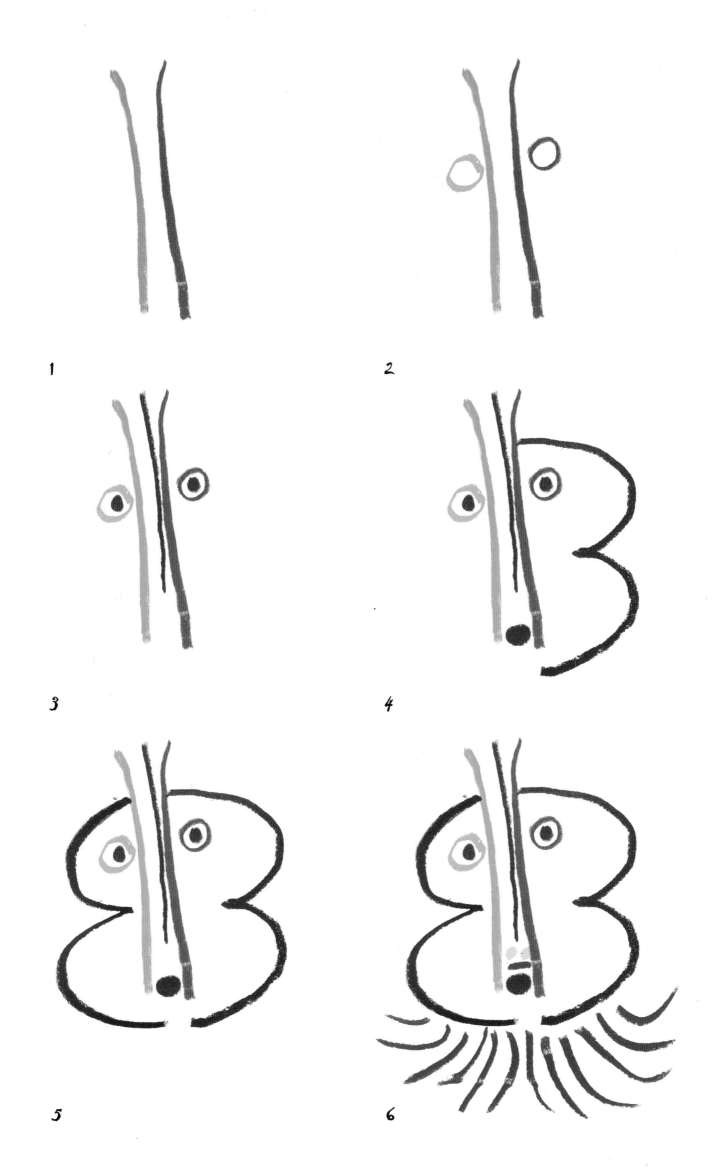

1

2

3

4

5

6

"Drawing is a way of telling stories."

1

2

3

4

5

6

1

2

3

4

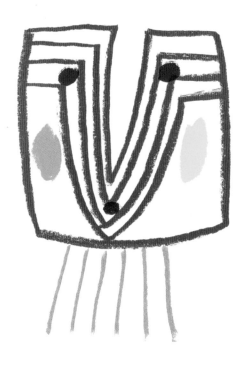

5

6

1

2

3

4

5

6

1

2

BIRDS

3

4

5

6

5.12.50. XI

"I don't paint what I see, I paint what I think."

1

2

3

4

5

6

"It's what we do that counts, not what we meant to do."

1

2

"I want to find a balance, one that I can snatch from the air."

3

4

1

2

3

4

5

6

"I have spent my whole life learning how to draw like a child."

1

2

3

4

5

6

"There comes a moment in life, when you have been working for a long time and the shapes seem to appear all by themselves…"

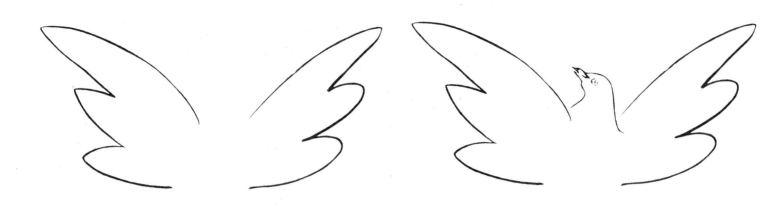

1

2

3

4

5

6

FLOWERS

1

2

3

4

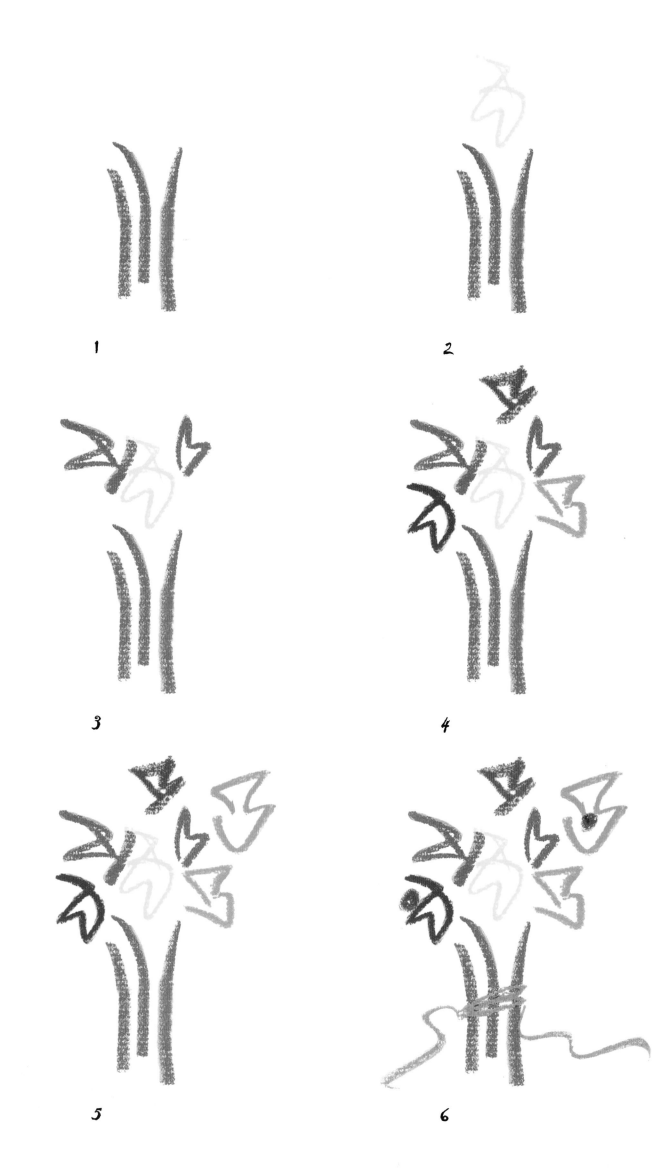

1

2

3

4

5

6

1

2

3

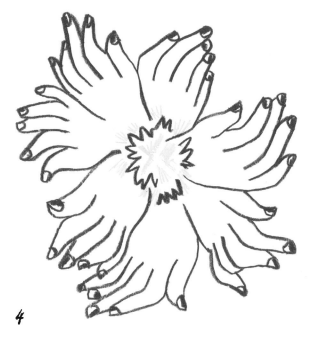

4

5

6

"The hand does everything, often without any intervention from the mind."

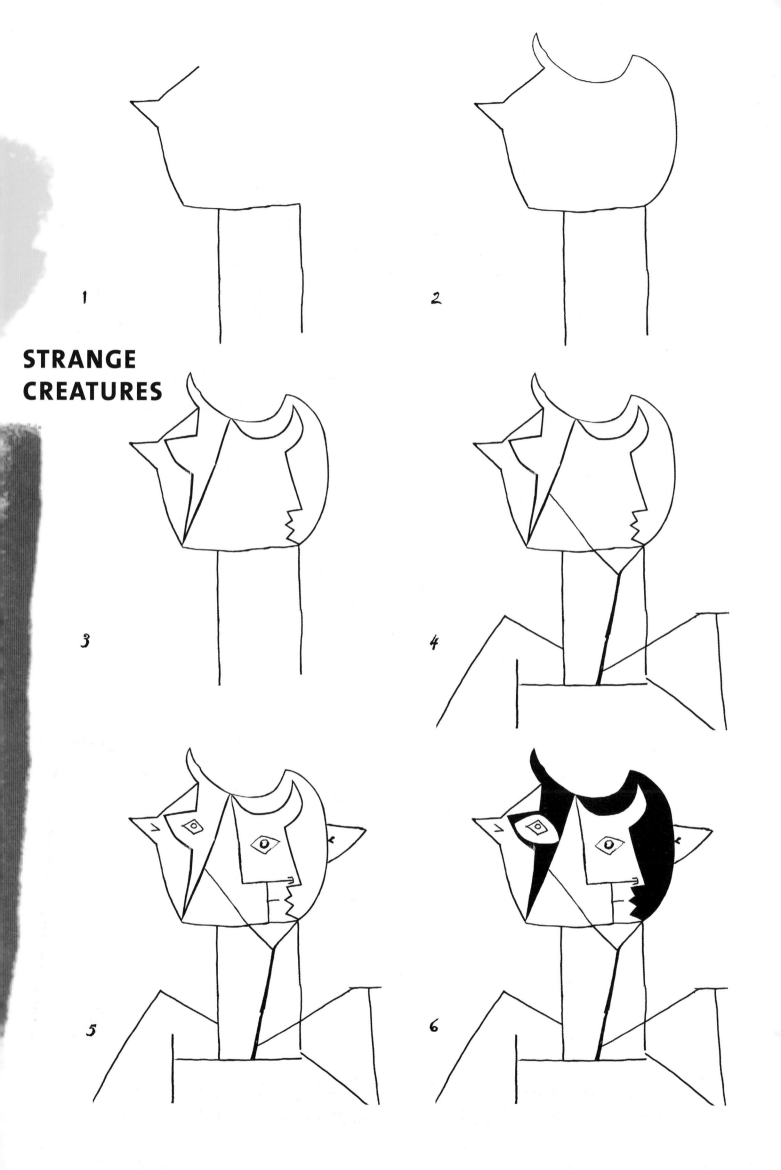

**STRANGE
CREATURES**

1

2

3

4

5

6

"The things I love all go into my paintings. Too bad for all the other things – they have to manage on their own."

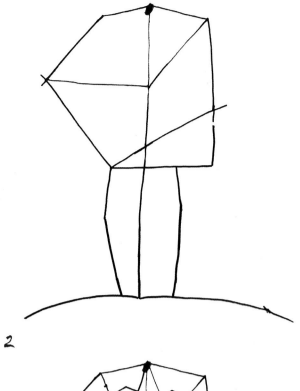

1

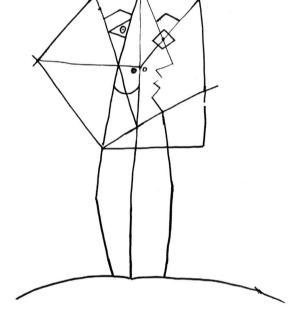

2

3

4

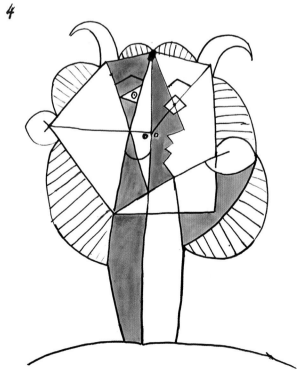

5

6

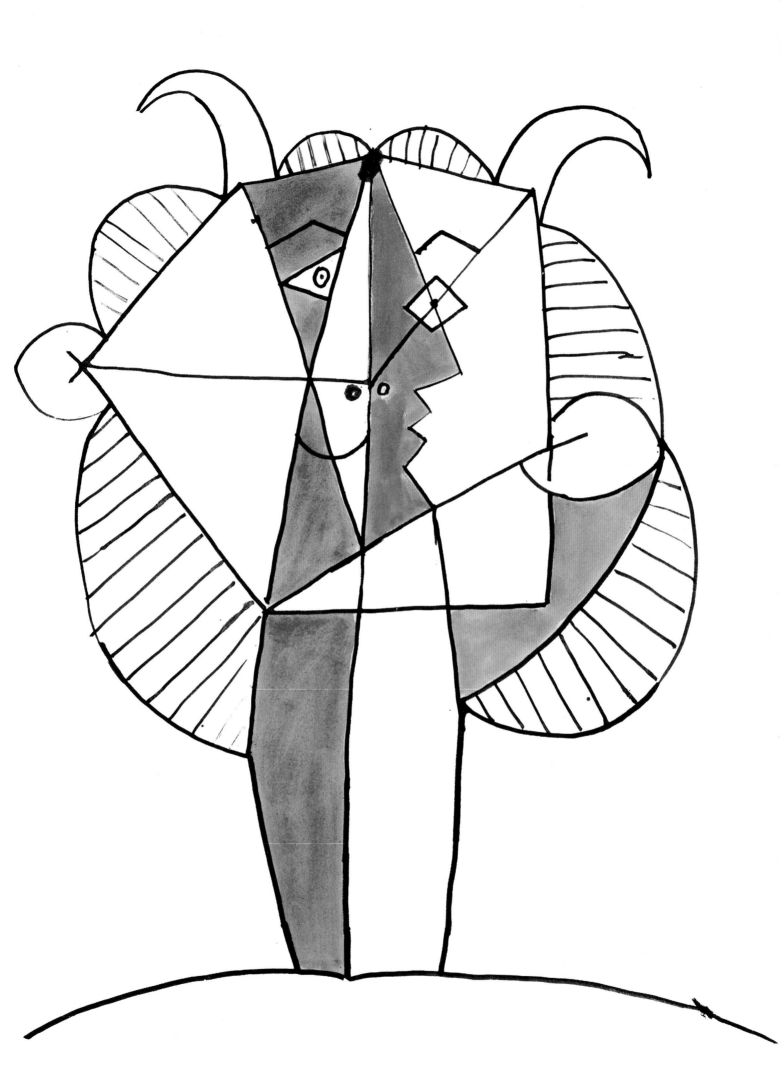

FROM A SINGLE LINE...

"Nothing is more difficult to draw than a line. No-one realises how much time you need to spend thinking about the line."

TABLE OF ILLUSTRATIONS AND PHOTOGRAPHIC ACKNOWLEDGEMENTS

This is my Heart

Woman in Love, or Arethusa

Prophetess

Washerwoman

Hector Fights

Narcissus' Mother

Priam the Ancient

King Kagpha

The Lady

Juan the Little Pigeon

Carnation

Flowers

Reproductions of coloured chalk drawings (1961) produced for the book *Loveless Fables (Gavilla de fabulas sin amor)* by Camilo José Cela, illustrated by Picasso. Musée Picasso, Paris. © Photo RMN / Th. Le Mage.

Pencil drawings taken from the book *The Face of Peace (Le Visage de la Paix)* by Paul Eluard, illustrated by Picasso, Éditions du Cercle d'Art, 1951.

The Face of Peace XI

The Face of Peace VIII

Two Owls, 1962, brown pencil on paper, 10.6 x 26.5cm. Private collection © Sotheby's Picture Library.

Dove of the World Festival of Youth and Students, coloured pencil, design for a scarf for the Moscow festival in 1957. © Bridgeman-Giraudon.

Dove of Peace, c. 1950, pastel, 23 x 31 cm. Musée d'Art Moderne de la Ville de Paris. © Photo RMN / Bulloz.

Illustration for the catalog of an exhibition of Picasso work at the Louise Leiris gallery, coloured lithograph 1957. Musée Picasso, Paris. © Photo RMN / M. Bellot.

Flower of Hands from *The Song of Flowers (Le chant des fleurs)* by Vladimir Pozner and Joris Ivens, illustrated by Picasso, 1955, coloured pencil on paper, 27 x 21cm. Private collection. © Bridgeman-Giraudon.

Cockerel, 1918, watercolour on paper, 22.6 x 27.8 cm. Musée Picasso, Paris. © Photo RMN.

Dog, 1918, lead pencil, 12.8 x 11.1 cm. Musée Picasso, Paris. © Photo RMN / Th. Le Mage.

Faun, 1946, watercolour and Chinese ink on paper, 66 x 51 cm. Musée Picasso, Antibes. © Bridgeman-Giraudon.

Collages – Watercolours – Gouaches at the Craven Gallery in Paris, June – September 1958, 1958, lithograph, 67 x 47 cm. Musée Picasso, Paris. © Photo RMN.

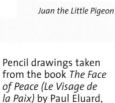

Paul Drawing, 1923, oil on canvas, 130 x 97 cm. Musée Picasso, Paris. © Photo RMN / J.-G. Berizzi.

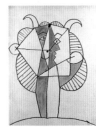

The Young Painter, 1972, oil on canvas, 130 x 162 cm. Musée Picasso, Paris. © Photo RMN / J.-G. Berizzi.

The Painter and the Child, 1969, oil on canvas, 130 x 195 cm. Musée Picasso, Paris. © Photo RMN / J.-G. Berizzi.

Claude Drawing with Françoise and Paloma, 1954, oil on canvas, 116 x 89 cm. Musée Picasso, Paris. © Photo RMN / J.-G. Berizzi.

At the La Californie villa in 1957. Photograph by René Burri. © Magnum Photos.

Draw with... Pablo Picasso copyright © Frances Lincoln Limited 2007
Text and design copyright © Gallimard Jeunesse 2006
Picasso artworks copyright © Succession Picasso 2006

This edition published in Great Britain in 2007 and the USA in 2008 by Frances Lincoln Children's Books, 4 Torriano Mews, Torriano Avenue, London NW5 2RZ
www.franceslincoln.com

First published under the title *Dessiner avec... Pablo Picasso* by Gallimard Jeunesse, Paris, France

English translation copyright © Antonia Parkin 2007

ISBN 978-1-84507-819-5   Printed in Italy   9 8 7 6 5 4 3 2 1